C000116294

ONE WAY OUT

by Montel Douglas

⫼SAMUEL FRENCH⫼

Copyright © 2023 by Montel Douglas
All Rights Reserved

ONE WAY OUT is fully protected under the copyright laws of the British Commonwealth, including Canada, the United States of America, and all other countries of the Copyright Union. All rights, including professional and amateur stage productions, recitation, lecturing, public reading, motion picture, radio broadcasting, television, online/digital production, and the rights of translation into foreign languages are strictly reserved.

ISBN 978-0-573-00034-8

concordtheatricals.co.uk
concordtheatricals.com

FOR AMATEUR PRODUCTION ENQUIRIES

UNITED KINGDOM AND WORLD
EXCLUDING NORTH AMERICA
licensing@concordtheatricals.co.uk
020-7054-7298

Each title is subject to availability from Concord Theatricals,
depending upon country of performance.

CAUTION: Professional and amateur producers are hereby warned that ONE WAY OUT is subject to a licensing fee. The purchase, renting, lending or use of this book does not constitute a licence to perform this title(s), which licence must be obtained from the appropriate agent prior to any performance. Performance of this title(s) without a licence is a violation of copyright law and may subject the producer and/or presenter of such performances to penalties. Both amateurs and professionals considering a production are strongly advised to apply to the appropriate agent before starting rehearsals, advertising, or booking a theatre. A licensing fee must be paid whether the title is presented for charity or gain and whether or not admission is charged.

This work is published by Samuel French, an imprint of Concord Theatricals Ltd.

Professional rights in this title are controlled by Concord Theatricals, Aldwych House, 71-91 Aldwych, London, WC2B 4HN

No one shall make any changes in this title for the purpose of production. No part of this book may be reproduced, stored in a retrieval system, scanned, uploaded, or transmitted in any form, by any means, now known or yet to be invented, including mechanical, electronic, digital, photocopying, recording, videotaping, or otherwise, without the prior written permission of the publisher. No one shall share this title, or part of this title, to any social media or file hosting websites.

The moral right of Montel Douglas to be identified as author of this work has been asserted in accordance with Section 77 of the Copyright, Designs and Patents Act 1988.

USE OF COPYRIGHTED MUSIC

A licence issued by Concord Theatricals to perform this play does not include permission to use the incidental music specified in this publication. In the United Kingdom: Where the place of performance is already licensed by the PERFORMING RIGHT SOCIETY (PRS) a return of the music used must be made to them. If the place of performance is not so licensed then application should be made to PRS for Music (www.prsformusic.com). A separate and additional licence from PHONOGRAPHIC PERFORMANCE LTD (www.ppluk.com) may be needed whenever commercial recordings are used. Outside the United Kingdom: Please contact the appropriate music licensing authority in your territory for the rights to any incidental music.

USE OF COPYRIGHTED THIRD-PARTY MATERIALS

Licensees are solely responsible for obtaining formal written permission from copyright owners to use copyrighted third-party materials (e.g., artworks, logos) in the performance of this play and are strongly cautioned to do so. If no such permission is obtained by the licensee, then the licensee must use only original materials that the licensee owns and controls. Licensees are solely responsible and liable for clearances of all third-party copyrighted materials, and shall indemnify the copyright owners of the play(s) and their licensing agent, Concord Theatricals Ltd., against any costs, expenses, losses and liabilities arising from the use of such copyrighted third-party materials by licensees.

IMPORTANT BILLING AND CREDIT REQUIREMENTS

If you have obtained performance rights to this title, please refer to your licensing agreement for important billing and credit requirements.

NO TABLE PRODUCTIONS

NO TABLE was assembled at Theatre Peckham as part of the government's Kickstart Scheme and is a collaboration between Guillaume Doussin, Ewa Dina, Montel Douglas, Nora Lempriere, and associate artist Emily Olum. All from a wide range of backgrounds and artistic practices, NO TABLE aims to create risk-taking work that uplifts the voices of the company through a playful and exploratory approach to theatre-making, embolden young creatives with artistic opportunities and knowledge of the industry, and challenge theatrical infrastructure asking the question: "Why ask for a seat at the table, and instead remove the table altogether?" While in residence at Theatre Peckham, the company created *No Table: Scraps*, *Eating Jeff*, and *One Way Out*.

NEW DIORAMA THEATRE

New Diorama Theatre is a pioneering studio venue in the heart of London.

Based on the corner of Regent's Park, over the last ten years New Diorama has been at the heart of a new movement in British theatre. New Diorama is the only venue in the UK entirely dedicated to providing a home for the country's best independent theatre companies and ensembles, and has established a national record as a trailblazer for early-career artist support.

"A genuine theatrical phenomenon – a miniature powerhouse." – *The Stage*

In 2022, New Diorama was named The Stage's Fringe Theatre Of The Year, for the second time in its short history; and in 2023 was awarded the inaugural Critics Circle Empty Space Venue Award. Since opening in 2010, New Diorama's work has also won four prestigious Peter Brook Awards; eleven Off West End Awards including Off West End Artistic Director of the Year; and The Stage's Innovation Prize.

"A must-visit destination for London theatregoers." – *Time Out*

Work commissioned and produced at New Diorama frequently tours nationally and internationally, including regular transfers Off-Broadway and co-curating New York's celebrated Brits Off Broadway Festival with 59E59 Theaters. The Stage 100, which charts power and influence across British Theatre, currently list New Diorama as the most influential independent studio theatre in the UK.

"A crucial part of the wider UK theatre ecology and an under-sung hero."
– *The Guardian*

In 2023, New Diorama achieved a further milestone with two original commissions transferring into London's West End. *For Black Boys Who Have Considered Suicide When The Hue Gets Too Heavy*, originally co-produced with Nouveau Riche and earning their artistic director Ryan Calais-Cameron an Olivier Award nomination for Best New Play, transferred first to the Royal Court Theatre before a limited, sell-out West End run at the Apollo Theatre. Alongside, *Operation Mincemeat*, an original New Diorama commission from musical theatre company Spitlip, transferred to the Fortune Theatre, where it has already extended its run several times.

"New Diorama has only been around for a decade but has already left a huge mark on the global theatre scene." – *WhatsOnStage*

www.newdiorama.com | @NewDiorama | New Diorama Theatre, 15-16 Triton Street, Regent's Place, London NW1 3BF.

UNTAPPED

UNDERBELLY | NEW DIORAMA THEATRE
CONCORD THEATRICALS | NOUVEAU RICHE

Originally developed in 2018 by New Diorama and Underbelly to discover and support emerging theatre makers at the Edinburgh Festival Fringe, the Untapped Award has established a remarkable record as a platform for bold new theatre by outstanding companies.

Over its 2018, 2019 and 2022 editions, the first three years of the Untapped Award have already provided a springboard for major Edinburgh Fringe premieres. Previous recipients have gone on to win three Fringe First Awards *This is Not a Show About Hong Kong* (Max Percy & Friends); *It's True, It's True, It's True* (Breach); *Dressed* (ThisEgg) and a Stage Edinburgh Award *Queens of Sheba* (Nouveau Riche). Winners have also gone on to secure major national and international tours following the festival (including Burnt Lemon's *Tokyo Rose*, Ugly Bucket's *Good Grief* and *Queens of Sheba* which most recently played at New York's Public Theater for the prestigious Under the Radar Festival, and adaptations for screen, with *It's True, It's True, It's True* broadcast on BBC television.

"The Untapped trio ranked among the best of the entire festival, proof that support from organisations like Underbelly and New Diorama can pay off in spades." – *WhatsOnStage*

For 2023, the award was relaunched and super-charged with support from new partners Concord Theatricals and previous winners Nouveau Riche, with the cash investment in each company doubled to £10,000 alongside an extensive paid-for support package and publication by Concord Theatricals under their UK imprint Samuel French Ltd.

Drawn from a nationwide talent search receiving a record one hundred and eighty submissions, the three 2023 winners are *Dugsi Dayz* by Side eYe, a Somali remix of *The Breakfast Club*; *One Way Out* by No Table Productions, a dynamic drama about young British Caribbeans' experiences of the Windrush crisis; and *It's A Motherf**king Pleasure* by FlawBored, a scathing satire on identity politics which asks "What if disabled people were out to make as much money as possible from the guilt of non-disabled, anxious people (like you)?"

CAST

DEVONTE – Shem Hamilton

Shem Hamilton trained at Theatre Peckham Rep 2019, GoHub and National Youth Theatre

Television credits include: *Black Cake* (Hulu), *StoneHouse* (ITV), *Small Axe* (BBC/Amazon)

Theatre credits include: *Sucker Punch* (National Theatre Tour); *One Way Out* (Theatre Peckham); *START*, (Theatre Peckham); *As You Like It* (The Cockpit Theatre); *Poles Apart* (Theatre 503)

TUNDE – Marcus Omoro

Marcus Omoro is an Actor from Peckham, London. He trained at Theatre Peckham Rep 2020 Open Door 2023 cohort member and begins Drama School in September 2023 at RADA (Royal Academy of Dramatic Art) to do a BA in Acting.

Theatre credits include: *No Man's Island* (Big House); *One Way Out* (Theatre Peckham); *Care* (Theatre Peckham).

SALIM – Adam Seridji

Adam Seridji is an Actor from South London. He trained at Theatre Peckham Rep 2020 & ALt. Club.

Television credits include: *Casualty* (BBC);

Theatre credits include: *One Way Out* (Theatre Peckham); *Care* (Theatre Peckham)

PAUL – Sam Pote

Sam is an Actor and Beatboxer from Ipswich, based in London. He came up through the New Wolsey's Young Company and the related multiple award-nominated theatre company, People You May Know, before then training at ALRA, graduating in 2021. He now regularly attends GoHub's workshops.

Television credits include: *DI Ray* (ITV)

Theatre credits include: *One Way Out* (Theatre Peckham)

Creative Team

MONTEL DOUGLAS – Writer & Director

Montel Douglas is a playwright & actor from London.

Douglas trained as an actor at Identity Drama School, Drama St Mary's Twickenham & Theatre Peckham Rep 2019.

One Way Out is his debut play. *One Way Out* has been supported by Talawa Theatre's introduction to playwriting group 2022, Soho Writer's lab 2022/23 & Royal Court introduction to playwriting group 2023. *One Way Out* was shortlisted for Pleasance Theatre Reserve Tryout 2023 & WINNER of UNTAPPED UNDERBELLY AWARD 2023.

Directing credits include: *Eating Jeff* (No Table / Camden People Theatre); *One Way Out* (Theatre Peckham)

Assistant Director credits include: *24* (Day) (Almeida Theatre); *The Light From Within* (New Wimbledon Theatre); *Anthem Live!* (Almeida Theatre).

Montel Douglas was the Creative Producer of *Black Joy*, Almeida Theatre, 2022.

Acting credits include: *Ransom* (CBS); *Code 404* (Sky One); *Casualty* (BBC); *Hamlet* (National theatre); *Run it Back* (Talawa Theatre Company); *Macbeth* (Orange Tree Theatre)

EMILY OLUM – Assistant Director

Born in London, Emily is of a rich and abundant Ugandan heritage, specifically Acholi. Emily studied Acting and World Theatre, under scholarship at Regent's University London and The New School for Drama in New York.

Acting credits include: *Essentially Black* (Soho Theatre), *Breathe* at (Seven Dials Playhouse / Tristan Bates) , *Anthem Live!* (Almeida Theatre)

Film credits include: *Playing With Fire*, *Yolk* (MYM)

In 2022, Emily became an associate artist of NO TABLE Productions.

One Way Out is Emily's debut as Assistant Director (and Dramaturg).

NORA LEMPRIERE – Creative Producer

Nora Lempriere (she/her) is a Community Artist and Stand Up Comedian from Lewisham, South East London. Previous TheatrePeckham Resident Artist (NO TABLE), Participation Coordinator at Southwark Playhouse, and Events Manager at the Vagina Museum, Nora has six jobs and six jokes.

CHARACTERS

DEVONTE – Eighteen, leader, Black, Jamaican. Playing age sixteen to eighteen, confident, troublesome. Impulsive.

TUNDE – Seventeen, Devonte's best friend, intelligent, black, Nigerian. Playing age sixteen to eighteen, shy, traditional.

PAUL – Seventeen, cockney, independent, Tunde's friend, English. Playing age sixteen to eighteen, laid back, nurturing. Also plays **IMMIGRATION OFFICER**.

SALIM – Eighteen, joker. Easily influenced, Muslim. From outside London, North African or South Asian. Playing age sixteen to eighteen, class clown. Actor must be of a Muslim background. Please adapt the text based on the actor's ethnicity.

SETTING

St Thomas Cathedral Sixth Form College.
Adventure Youth Club.

TIME

The play is set in present-day South London.

AUTHOR'S NOTES

A dash (–) is used to indicate an interruption and a slash (/) denotes an overlap in dialogue.

Dialogue side by side is to be spoken at the same time.

Pauses and silences are important but are not fixed. Each pause and silence should be considered at that moment. However, more often than not, a silence should be longer than a pause.

A swooshing sound is to indicate a new day.

migrant
noun
A person who moves from one place to another, especially in order to find work or better living conditions.

immigrant
noun
A person who comes to live permanently in a foreign country.

ACKNOWLEDGEMENTS

In Loving memory of Keith Mckay
Who passed away from Kidney Faliure
1956 -2022

This play is dedicated to Dominque 'Berta' Cameron, who in 2012 was deported to Clarendon, Jamaica, aged nineteen, after living in the UK for ten years.

"Cuz, to tell yuh the truth, mi could only see one way out."

Thank you to all who have supported me & helped make this project come to life. Myself & NO TABLE would like to thank;

Theatre Peckham, Southwark Playhouse, Emily Aboud, Suzann Mclean, Toby Clarke, Tyrell Williams, Talawa Theate, David Gilbert, Michelle Matherson, Streatham Space Project, Blue Elephant Theatre, Vagina Museum, Soho Theatre, Lakesha Arie-Angelo, Underbelly, Pleasance, New Diorama Theatre, Nouveau Riche, Sarah Jodan Verghese,
Ryan Calais Cameron
& a special thank you to
Mark Oliver (who played Leroy in Theatre Peckham adaptation of *One Way Out*).

Foreword

In the heart of London, where dreams come alive,
A tale of courage and resilience shall thrive,
Of a soul who faced deportation's cruel sting,
Yet found strength to soar on Hope's golden wing.

From Jamaica's shores, a land steeped in grace,
He ventured forth, seeking a brighter embrace,
Opportunity whispered, a promise so grand,
London's allure beckoned, a destiny unplanned.

Without passport in hand, he crossed oceans wide,
Leaving behind a world he had known with pride,
But the price he would pay, he couldn't foresee,
The loss of his roots, his beloved family.

Loneliness embraced him, like a shadow's caress,
As he yearned for the warmth of a friend's tenderness,
Yet in this vast city, where strangers abound,
He discovered a love that would astound.

In the heart of London, he found a love so true,
A love that would attempt to mend what deportation once blew,
For in her eyes, he saw a reflection of his own,
A love like a river, forever to be known.

And in their hearts, a seed of hope was sown,
A life yet unborn, a future brightly shown,
For their love transcended borders and strife,
Embracing the promise of a brand-new life.

Through the trials they faced, hand in hand,
They built a sanctuary on this foreign land,
With each passing day, their love did grow,
Like the river Thames, with an ever-steady flow.

Once he knew the decision was final,
Each choice became crucially vital
As for his actions, they need to be taken for account.
But to tell you the truth, there was only One Way Out.

ACT ONE

Detention

(January.)

*(Four **BOYS** were previously play-fighting on their lunch break and an amalgamation of ties, blazers and sweaty teens tussle through the space and a playful push results in a broken window in the school building. The tannoy makes an announcement. All four **BOYS** have been called into the headteacher's office separately to discuss what has happened and to decide their appropriate punishments.)*

*(Four chairs facing down the stage. Seated left to right, **PAUL**, **TUNDE**, **DEVONTE**, **SALIM**.)*

DEVONTE. What do you mean I'm not going to amount to anything, Miss?

SALIM. Grades? Why are we talking about my grades?

TUNDE. They are my friends, Miss. I can't just leave them.

PAUL. Joint enterprise. Are you wearing a new perfume?

DEVONTE. My attitude stinks?

SALIM. I didn't do it.

TUNDE. It's clear to see that I had nothing to do with this.

PAUL. Smells nice.

DEVONTE. Stinks? And you're the one saying I ain't gonna achieve anything.

(**DEVONTE** *kisses his teeth.*)

PAUL. Lemme guess, Yves Saint Laurent perfume Mon Paris.

(**PAUL** *blows a kiss.*)

SALIM. I ain't snitching. Those are my boys.

DEVONTE. Na, Miss you're violating.

PAUL. I couldn't possibly be the one to cause a scene. I mean, look at me. *(Cheeky smile.)*

DEVONTE. I didn't touch him.

TUNDE. I didn't break the window. It was...

PAUL. Just a push.

SALIM. Come on, Miss, we were just mucking around. Just a few little scruffles. None of us are even hurt.

TUNDE. There wasn't a substantial amount of force.

DEVONTE. Can't you see I'm the one in pain.

(**TUNDE** *more like a gentle nudge.*)

CCTV? Kmt. You ain't got no evidence.

TUNDE. I'm sorry, it was very irresponsible of me.

SALIM. Well, we were all involved yeah.

PAUL. Can we come to some sort of agreement?

DEVONTE. Excluded!! For what!

TUNDE. I tried to calm everyone down.

SALIM. Detention!!

PAUL. Scot-free!?! See I knew you were my favourite teacher.

DEVONTE. You've always had something against me.

PAUL. Okay, sorry miss. It won't happen again.

TUNDE. Two thousand word-essay, but Miss, I didn't do anything. I was just a bystander. I promise I'm not lying. Just, just rethink this essay, please. I've got so much on right now and –

DEVONTE. I don't think this is fair.

SALIM. Miss I think you need to release some tension because you're taking the P. I. DOUBLE –

TUNDE. Excuse me miss, I'm sorry just please don't tell my parents.

PAUL. Once again sorry for the inconvenience.

DEVONTE. Cool. It is what it is.

TUNDE. May I go now?

> *(End of discussion with the teacher. Sixth form Corridors, Lunchtime.* **BOYS** *are walking.)*

PAUL. Phew! We got out of that one lads.

SALIM. Who's We? I got detention all next week.

PAUL. Soz yeah!

TUNDE. You guys didn't say anything did you?

SALIM. Course not.

PAUL. I just said what she wanted to hear.

TUNDE. What about you Devonte?

DEVONTE. I got excluded.

TUNDE, SALIM & PAUL. Excluded!!

SALIM. Rah. How come?

PAUL. You're kidding.

TUNDE. I just got told to do a two thousand-word essay. That's all.

DEVONTE. Well clearly Miss Wilson wants you to work on your strengths. And mine is not in this place.

SALIM. D, come on man, don't say things like that.

DEVONTE. Agh my mum's gonna kill me.

SALIM. We'll tell Aunty Barbara that Miss Wilson was lying.

DEVONTE. She said there was evidence that I started it.

TUNDE. But it was me.

DEVONTE. Exactly.

SALIM. Hold up, how can she get both of you mixed up. You look nothing alike. That's a bit rac / -ist

TUNDE & DEVONTE. / Is this guy for real?

PAUL. Salim, I think what Miss was trying to get at is, to her it doesn't matter who did it. We didn't take responsibility for it.

DEVONTE. One person getting excluded isn't owning up to responsibility, is it?

TUNDE. Just say it as it is.

PAUL. It's because...because you're...black AIR FORCES. You're wearing black Air Forces.

DEVONTE. I can't deal with you sometimes.

SALIM. Hang on a minute, how do I get a week's worth of detention and he gets an essay?

PAUL. Do you wanna do an essay?

SALIM. Certainly not but –

PAUL. Right then. D. How long are you gone for then?

DEVONTE. Two weeks.

TUNDE, SALIM & PAUL. Two weeks!

TUNDE. Devonte, Sorry about that man. We didn't mean for you to get in trouble.

DEVONTE. Na it's cool. That teacher was out to get me, ever since me and Salim locked that OFSTED inspector in the lunch hall with a broom.

SALIM. They were screaming "let me out let me out ah". Good times.

(**DEVONTE & SALIM** *spud.*)

DEVONTE. I guess it's Karma init. What goes around...

SALIM. Comes back around.

PAUL. *(Starts singing the first two lines of Justin Timberlake's "What Goes Around...Comes Around".*)

DEVONTE & SALIM. Wahgwarn for my man!

(Both laugh.)

(**PAUL** *stops.*)

TUNDE. I just didn't want to get in trouble with my parents, that's all. Mum's been stressing bare recently, got a new job at the Home Office, constantly working overtime & hardly ever around anymore. But it pays well so. If I stay out of trouble, they're finally letting me have a birthday party.

(**BOYS** *react.*)

ALL. Ayyeeeeee!

TUNDE. This gonna be THE party of the summer mandem, the big eighteenth, right before I head off to Uni. We got Jollof rice, pounded yam, Suya, chicken wings, and a Nigerian Fanta with no ice.

---

* A licence to produce *One Way Out* does not include a performance license for any third-party or copyrighted music. Licensees should create an original composition or use music in the public domain. For further information, please see the Music Use Note on page iii.

*(The **BOYS** sing the first two lines of J Hus - "Friendly".*)*

TUNDE. I'm not tryna ruin my chances.

SALIM. You mean your chances with Michaela.

(They laugh.)

TUNDE. Shut up Salim, who doesn't like Michaela?

SALIM, DEVONTE & PAUL. True!!!

DEVONTE. *(To **TUNDE**.)* It's alright bro, how many years have I had your back?

TUNDE. Yeah you have. Thanks for not snitching on me.

DEVONTE. You owe me.

(They do their special handshake and embrace.)

SALIM. Yeah Yeah Yeah, enough with all that lovey dovey stuff. The real question is... Who's even going to your party?

*(**SALIM** runs off laughing.)*

*(**DEVONTE** puts his arm around **TUNDE**.)*

DEVONTE. Don't worry bro, I'll make sure the whole college comes to your party.

TUNDE. It's cool, I've already handed out flyers.

---

* A licence to produce *One Way Out* does not include a performance licence for J Hus - "Friendly". The publisher and author suggest that the licensee contact PRS to ascertain the music publisher and contact such music publisher to license or acquire permission for performance of the song. If a licence or permission is unattainable for J Hus - "Friendly", the licensee may not use the song in *One Way Out* but should create an original composition in a similar style or use a similar song in the public domain. For further information, please see the Music and Third-Party Materials Use Note on page iii.

*(**TUNDE** smiles. **DEVONTE** drops his head in defeat.)*

PAUL. Well, I got somewhere that would make us all happy?

TUNDE. Where?

ALL. YOUTH CLUB!!!!

Adventure Youth Club

SALIM. Devonte I can't believe your mum owns a youth club. That's so sick!

PAUL. Yeah way cooler than your uncle Abdul's off-licence.

SALIM. Oi!

DEVONTE. She doesn't 'own' it, Mum's just the manager.

TUNDE. Is Aunty Barbara in today?

DEVONTE. Nah, mum's still not feeling well, Doctors have put her on this new dialysis treatment.

PAUL. Sorry to hear that, D. What's Dialysis?

SALIM. So wait you comforted my man, these times you didn't even know what it is?

　　　　(**SALIM** *laughs hysterically.*)

PAUL. I didn't wanna ruin the moment. I swear Salim you can be so insensitive sometimes, you know that.

TUNDE. Kidney Failure. Aunty Barbara's got Kidney failure. so the doctors have put her on this machine (dialysis) to help aid with her treatment.

PAUL. Oh thanks Tunde.

　　　　(**TUNDE & PAUL** *spud.*)

PAUL. D, if there's anything you need, we got you bro.

DEVONTE. Love Mandem, it's cool though. Mum just makes me & my little sister carry all the cardboard boxes to the recycling bin. I swear the neighbours must think I'm an Amazon delivery driver.

TUNDE. Must be hard trying to to run a youth club, especially with an illness.

SALIM. Yeah my uncle said if you need anything, plasters, paracetamol or even magazines to occupy her time, it's on the house.

DEVONTE. I appreciate it mandem, besides Ricky, got it all covered.

PAUL. My guy Ricky!!!!!

TUNDE. Ricky is such a cool guy.

DEVONTE. When I grow up I wanna be respected like Ricky.

SALIM. Respect from seventeen/eighteen-year-old boys?

PAUL, DEVONTE & TUNDE. Shut up Salim.

DEVONTE. Ricky is the coolest youth worker, imagine, this guy allows us to play on FIFA fifteen minutes extra. "Gooaaaaallllll!!"

PAUL. The guy will buy pizza for everyone and ask you what toppings you want. Pepperoni and extra mushrooms!!

TUNDE. The guy that will sit you down and help you decide on your university choices. "Oxbridge? You think so?"

DEVONTE, TUNDE & PAUL. *Ricky is that guy.*

SALIM. Whatever. Bet, I beat you all on Fifa.

DEVONTE. Three NILL WIPE WASH!!!

TUNDE. I'm gonna smoke you all.

(Lights change. / Swoosh sound.)

Adventure Youth Club 2

(New day. **BOYS** *are now spaced around the space, doing their maths homework.)*

PAUL. Ah this is boring, how am I supposed to know what the *sin* formula is.

SALIM. I don't know why you thought you could handle A-level maths.

PAUL. I dunno, I thought numbers yeah that would be easy. Why are there so many letters? I mean, who even needs to use trigo trignong –

TUNDE. Trigonometry?

DEVONTE. Architects, Construction workers and Cartographers. Them man all use the Pythagorean theorem, to help aid the construction of stable buildings and bridges, init.

(The **BOYS** *are surprised at Devonte's response.)*

(Pause.)

What? You lot didn't know that?

SALIM. Are we all going to ignore that Tunde's words came out of Devonte's mouth.

DEVONTE. Shut up Salim. I'm not stupid you know.

TUNDE. Impressive...

PAUL. What's a cartographer?

SALIM. Someone who creates cartoons. You eediat!!

*(***DEVONTE*** drops his head in defeat.)*

DEVONTE. No, Salim. It's someone who produces maps.

TUNDE. With this knowledge, I don't know why you haven't applied for university yet.

DEVONTE. Uni? Do you think after this exclusion any university would take me?

TUNDE. I'm serious, you'll be able to maximise your potential. And D, I said I was sorry about that.

DEVONTE. It's cool. Anyways, I can't just pack up and leave my mum to go to another side of the country, can I?

TUNDE. But what about *your* future? We ain't going to be young forever you know.

DEVONTE. Ricky said once I get my grades I can come and work here, if I like.

The truth is none of us can predict the future no matter how hard are we try.

PAUL. Actually, I'm trying out this new trick, which can predict which card you have. I think that's pretty psychic if you ask me.

SALIM. *(To* **PAUL**.*)* Not now.

TUNDE. There's Uni options in London.

SALIM. That's true D.

TUNDE. How about you study to become a nephrologist? Look I know you don't have a clue what these doctors are saying when you go to them appointments. Plus Aunty Barbara, is just going to say it's fine. She don't want you to worry.

SALIM. Just apply bro.

TUNDE. You could change your life. And possibly –

(**DEVONTE** *gives him the look.*)

Most certainly change your mum's.

(**DEVONTE** *considers.*)

TUNDE. D, we're just tryna look out for you bro, as much as you do for us.

DEVONTE. Yeah I know.

>   *(Pause.)*

You really think Uni could be for me?

TUNDE. Course bro. Plus man's gonna need a wingman when we go to all them Uni parties.

DEVONTE. Yeah I've heard they're lit!

TUNDE. Exactly, so what d'you say? Deadline's tomorrow.

>   *(**DEVONTE** ponders.)*

Who's the smartest guy I know?

TUNDE, PAUL & SALIM. Devonte!!

PAUL. Who's the coolest kid I KNOW?

TUNDE, PAUL & SALIM. Devonte!!

SALIM. Who's gonna get that dough?

TUNDE, PAUL & SALIM. Devonte!!

>   *(The **BOYS** repeatedly chant "Devonte" as words of encouragement.)*

DEVONTE. Alright, Alright... Cool, I'll apply

TUNDE. YESSSSSS!

DEVONTE. But only if you man help me with the application.

TUNDE. Calm, I'll even get Ricky to look over your personal statement. Lemme go ask him for a laptop.

>   *(**TUNDE** exits.)*

PAUL. Well, I don't wanna go to Uni. My dream is to be a Magician.

(Rest of the **BOYS** *laugh.)*

SALIM. I'd advise you don't quit your day job.

PAUL. Haha very funny. Don't have one.

DEVONTE. Magician? Is he being serious?

*(***SALIM*** checks bulletin board.)*

SALIM. Oi Justin Timberlake [Paul], you could do ballroom dancing as well. It says they've got a class here every Thursday night.

(They laugh hysterically again.)

PAUL. Shut up Salim. Watch me. I'm gonna be a bad boy Magician.

(Attempts to do a trick and fails.)

*(***TUNDE*** enters with laptop.)*

TUNDE. Guys, I leave you for two minutes

*(***DEVONTE & SALIM*** put their hands up in surrender.)*

PAUL. Ah yeah, alright watch this.

*(***PAUL*** takes the stage and presents a magic trick with cards. The ***BOYS*** go wild as they can't believe it was a success. They are baffled.)*

SALIM. OOOOHHHH MYYYY DAYYYYYYYYSSSSSSS!!! NAAAAAAA HOW DID YOU DO THAT?

DEVONTE. Can't lie that was sick still.

TUNDE. That can't be real, there must be something behind it.

*(***TUNDE*** puts his hands in the sign of a crucifix.)*

SALIM. Course it's real bruv, it's magic!!

PAUL. Told yah.

TUNDE. Can we just get back to work!!

      (Pause.)

  Name?

DEVONTE. Devonte Troy Miller.

SALIM. Date of Birth?

DEVONTE. Eighth May 2005.

PAUL. Predicted grades?

DEVONTE. B, C, D.

SALIM. You sure you wanna put that in?

      *(The **BOYS** ponder.)*

BOYS. Hmmm.

TUNDE. A, B, B?

BOYS. YEAAAAHH!!

PAUL. Nationality?

DEVONTE. British. *(Beat.)* Jamaican.

PAUL. They don't have dual nationality on here.

SALIM. Just put where you were born.

DEVONTE. Jamaica.

PAUL. I didn't know you were born in Jamaica.

DEVONTE. You didn't need to know.

PAUL. So how come you don't have an accent.

DEVONTE. *(Speaks in Patois.)* Bikaaz unnuh people wouldnt bi able tuh undastan mi.

PAUL. Rassclart! *(English accent.)*

(**DEVONTE** *gives him 'the look'.*)

Sorry. *(Pause.)* My yute.

DEVONTE. Oi.

(**DEVONTE** *chases* **PAUL**.)

TUNDE. Can we get back to work?

DEVONTE & PAUL. Sorry.

TUNDE. Thank you. Right, passport number?

DEVONTE. Who knows that off the top of their head?

BOYS. Ah come on D!

PAUL. You must have a picture of it or something.

DEVONTE. Psshh! Never seen mine.

PAUL. You know the burgundy thingy, well since BREXIT and all that nonsense the blue one.

DEVONTE. I know what it is, Mum just handles all that stuff. Always goes on about *(Patois.)* "Mi need to keep it ina safe place".

PAUL. What like keep it under the mattress.

DEVONTE. Yeah most likely to be fair.

SALIM. So D, you've never left the country?

DEVONTE. Barely ever left South London.

SALIM. Oh my dayssss!

PAUL. Gordon Bennett!

TUNDE. Father God, please get my brother out the hood. In Jesus name Amen.

SALIM. Insha'Allah Ameen, even me, at least, I've been to Bradford. Gotta do better Devonte.

DEVONTE. You man chill, I've never seen the need to. Why leave when you've got everything here? Morley's, Youth Club. Goal pitches. Bagel King! Sounds like paradise to me. Plus Mum said we will go on holiday when she gets better with her kidney.

SALIM. Ah Whatever D, at least go Brighton beach or something.

DEVONTE. *(To* **TUNDE**.*)* I'll fill out that part when I get home.

PAUL. So...are we gonna be able to finish it in time?

TUNDE. There's ways to get around it. It's minor. I got this.

> (**TUNDE** *spuds* **DEVONTE** *then types and completes the application.)*

And sent. Mandem, we are looking at Devonte Miller, the guy who's just applied to university!!!!

> (**BOYS** *cheer.)*

BOYS. Devonte! Devonte! Devonte!

> *(Lights change. / Swoosh sound.)*

Adventure Youth Club 3

(May. Some of the **BOYS** *are revising and others are playing games, in the Youth Club.)*

SALIM. What about you T? What do you wanna be?

TUNDE. Something in a suit, I guess. I know that would make my parents proud, for sure. An accountant would be good. And yourself?

SALIM. I want to be a franchise owner of many local off-licenses.

PAUL. Ain't your family kinda like that already?

SALIM. Well yeah. A few of my uncles own their shop. But imagine owning five or ten or even one hundred across the city. I would be rolling in the money. I could buy a car, a mansion, a yacht, get bare gyal, you name it.

But when I bring this up to my uncle he's always like, "Salim greed is not a good trait to have." How is that greed? When the White man owns about seven or eight properties on the same road, no one calls him greedy.

PAUL. I don't own any /

SALIM. / They come in with their high rent charges, newly furnished apartments that, let's be real, none of us can live in.

Boy! Don't get me started on their fancy independent coffee shops. Come on now, we don't need three of them on the same road. /

TUNDE. / I just want a pattie bro.

BOYS. PREACH!!

SALIM. So the next time my uncle decides to school me again, I'm going to tell him that it's not greed. I see it as an ambition for me and my people.

(Pause.)

TUNDE. Well said Salim.

PAUL. Are we allowed to have an eighteen-year-old prime minister, because I'm not really trusting this Rishi Sunak guy in power.

DEVONTE. Rishi Affi go!

(All the **BOYS** *laugh.)*

(Beat.)

PAUL. Seeing as you man are willing to help the community, are you willing to help a friend with their maths homework?

DEVONTE. *(Smiles.)* You're a wasteman you know that, *(Beat.)* give it here.

Dream

(We see **DEVONTE** *in a dream state, we hear flashbacks to his days as a child. Rainbow in the sky. Children playing freely in the distance. This puts a smile on* **DEVONTE***'s face. A youthful woman calls his name "Devonte, come to me". His physical state is trying grasp onto this call, however the more he reaches the more difficult it gets. As the struggle increases the call of "Devonte" begins to sound urgent, opposite from the* **BOYS***' chants.* **DEVONTE** *begins to hyperventilate as he continues to search for the call. He awakens. Out of breath, almost shaken, as if a dream turned in to a nightmare.)*

Results Day

(School bell rings. Present-day, South London. August thirteenth, A-level/BTEC Results Day. Group of teens, queuing up to collect their results. Nervous.)

PAUL. Oi lads, who would have thought that us nob-heads would be getting a proper qualification.

(**TUNDE** *is nervously waiting.*)

SALIM. I'm just lucky that I made it to the end. D, how you feeling?

DEVONTE. Composed.

PAUL. Tunde... Mr. Brain Box.

SALIM. Oi South London's Einstein.

TUNDE. Shhh...

(Silence.)

Just have to wait patiently that's all.

PAUL. Mate, this isn't GCSE, you will get a job in the future I promise yah!

TUNDE. It's not about that. I want to get into my first choice.

SALIM. Chill man, besides if worse comes to worst, you can come and work at my Uncle's shop.

PAUL. No offence Salim but none of us want to be stacking shelves for the rest of our life. We all just need to relax. My dad says education isn't everything. It's about life experience, going out there in the big world, exploring.

SALIM. Easy for you to say. You aren't going to have aunties and uncles waiting at your doorstep, who have come from Bradford to hear the 'great news'.

PAUL. 'Great news' ha! Come to think of it, when I got my GCSE results no one cared.

> *(Impersonates his dad.)*

"As long as you know how to spell your name and count money, you'll be alright son." I'm only good at one of those things.

SALIM. What are we going to do to celebrate?

PAUL. Nandos?

SALIM. Sounds sick!

PAUL. Yeah cheap as chips.

> **(DEVONTE & TUNDE** *become visibly nervous.)*

SALIM. Don't know why you-lot are sweating it. This college isn't going to take your picture and plaster it on the wall for being an outstanding student.

TUNDE. You don't know that.

PAUL. Einstein has returned.

SALIM. You know it's true.

DEVONTE. Aye Tunde, See you on the other side, yeah?

TUNDE. See you on the other side, my brother.

> **(TUNDE & DEVONTE** *hail up each other, as sign to send good luck to one another.)*

> *(Beat.)*

SALIM. One small step for man...

PAUL. One giant step for the mandem.

> **(PAUL & SALIM** *spud and laugh histerically.)*

TUNDE. Shhh! I'm next.

(They all go silent.)

*(**BOYS** step forward and collect their results simultaneously. They stare at each other taking one large deep breath, as their future awaits for them behind a brown envelope.)*

SALIM. Guys, let's just go to Adventure Youth Club, chill out there and when the time is right, we can open all our results.

PAUL & DEVONTE. Yeah Yeah.

TUNDE. Yeah nah sorry guys. Mummy got to see these results first. Imagine, she's taken a day off, just to hear the news. Catch you man ina bit though yeah!

*(**TUNDE** exits.)*

SALIM. Snake!!

*(**PAUL** rips opened his envelope first. His eyes scatter down the page, the rest of the **BOYS** are intrigued to hear Paul's results.)*

PAUL. Salim.

SALIM. Yeah.

(Pause.)

PAUL. Has your Uncle got vacancies?

*(**DEVONTE** laughs, **SALIM** comforts **PAUL**.)*

No More Youth

*(Distracted, **DEVONTE** is looking at his phone to see to his if he got into university. The UCAS application states "Rejected". Disappointed and startled. We see a confused look on his face as he approaches the Youth Club.)*

(Outside Adventure Youth Club.)

PAUL. Erm Salim we are here now, and my grades didn't change.

SALIM. Na, yours ain't changing still. It looks like nobody is here.

DEVONTE. What do you mean? Someone is always here.

*(**SALIM** tries to pull the door.)*

PAUL. It's closed.

DEVONTE. Oi, hello!! Is anyone here?

*(**SALIM** reads a sign on the door.)*

SALIM. "Due to redevelopment in the local area, Adventure Youth Centre will be closing down permanently at the end of next week. The Youth Club will only be used for pre-booked events until closure... Our apologies, From Adventure Team."

PAUL. Is that it?

SALIM. I think so.

DEVONTE. It can't be, someone must be playing a prank. HELLO! Ricky!!. Come on man.

*(**DEVONTE** tries to call his mum [Aunty Barbara].)*

DEVONTE. *(On the phone.)* Hello, is this Royal Free Hospital? Could you put me through to the Urology department please. Would like to speak to Barbara Miller, it's an emergency.

She's a patient there, yes, thank you, I'll hold.

PAUL. D...D. just forget it.

DEVONTE. *(To* **SALIM.***)* Na! Man Na!

Argh, are you going to put me through or not?

SALIM. D...Paul's right, let's just forget it.

DEVONTE. Shut up, Salim.

(To phone.) No I wasnt talking to you. Sorry could you just...

(Phone hangs up.)

*(***DEVONTE** *evokes frustration.)*

PAUL. D...Chill /

DEVONTE. / How can I chill, it's alright for you lot.

SALIM. It's not that deep, at least we will still be able to have Tunde's party here. After that we can just go to another one in a different ends.

DEVONTE. You just don't get it, do you. My mum just lost her job. Can't just 'go to different ends', can we?

*(***DEVONTE** *confronts* **SALIM.***)*

PAUL. D has got a point.

SALIM. But bro you are going to have to find another way to occupy your time.

PAUL. We all have to.

DEVONTE. Kmt!

(Out of anger, **DEVONTE** *decides to rip his results paper up.)*

SALIM. Oi what did you do that for!

PAUL. Are you bloody insane mate!

DEVONTE. I didn't get in!

SALIM. What?

> *(Beat.)*

DEVONTE. I got rejected. What's the point of even giving myself hope and looking at these results, When I got more important things to be worrying about.

SALIM. I'm so sorry D –

> *(**TUNDE** enters.)*

TUNDE. *(Excitedly.)* Yoooooooooooooooooooooooooooo. Guess who got in to their first choice!

> *(**PAUL** and **SALIM** read the room.)*

In three years time Babatunde Jesufikunayomi Adebayo will be the new accountant from The 'Peckham'.

> *(**TUNDE** goes his special handshake with the **BOYS**. **DEVONTE** doesn't respond. **TUNDE** is too excited to notice.)*

DEVONTE. Congrats.

TUNDE. Thanks Mandem. *(To **DEVONTE**.)* Oh yeah saw your sister on the way here. Told me to give this you. Looks important, could be from your Uni bro.

> *(Hands **DEVONTE** a letter, **DEVONTE** rejects the letter.)*

> *(**TUNDE** is taken aback.)*

> *(**TUNDE** sees and picks up the torn results paper.)*

TUNDE. *(Shocked, [potentially in Yoruba].)* What did you that for?

DEVONTE. I ain't got time for your lectures. Need to go speak to my mum.

> *(**TUNDE** blocks **DEVONTE***'s way to leave.)*

TUNDE. I don't understand. Devonte we're trying to help you. Why don't you help yourself for a change? This ain't it.

DEVONTE. Help myself? All I do is help people and what do I get. Nothing.

SALIM. Na D stop now man.

TUNDE. Na let him carry on. He's always got excuses.

DEVONTE. Excuses, I'd applied for Uni, to do a course that YOU convince me to do and I got rejected. How is that excuses?

TUNDE. But why though? Have you even open –

DEVONTE. I don't care. Now move out my way, because I've got places to be. Or are you gonna tell my mum she's out of a job?

TUNDE. I see you've given up already.

> *(**TUNDE** lets **DEVONTE** pass.)*

If I was your mum I'd be disappointed in you.

> *(Beat.)*

DEVONTE. What did you just say?

> *(**DEVONTE** punches **TUNDE**.)*

> *(**PAUL** and **SALIM** try to break it up, **PAUL** goes for **DEVONTE**, **SALIM** goes for **TUNDE**.)*

SALIM. That's a violation.

PAUL. Tunde you don't understand –

SALIM. D, all he's saying is he wants the best for you that's all.

DEVONTE. SHUT UP SALIM, haven't you got to go to your uncle's shop or something? I got excluded because of you... Man gets a fancy piece of paper and all of sudden they switch on you.

    (**SALIM** *and* **PAUL** *try to break up the fight.* **TUNDE** *pushes* **SALIM** *off him.*)

TUNDE. You know what, forget it. You just want to throw your life away, go ahead. That's the last time I do anything again for you!

    (**TUNDE** *throws the letter on the floor.*)

    (**TUNDE** *leaves.*)

    (*Silence.*)

SALIM. I'm gone.

PAUL. Where are you going?

SALIM. To see if my uncle needs help at the shop. Apparently, I'm needed there.

    (**SALIM** *goes.*)

    (*Beat.*)

PAUL. D, you alright?

    (*Beat.*)

    (*Paul's phone rings, it's his Dad.*)

PAUL. Ah Dad, is everything alright? How many this time? Yeah, I'll pick em up for yah.

    (**PAUL** *hangs up.*)

Salim wait up.

(PAUL exits.)

(On stage on his own DEVONTE opens the letter. It's from the Home Office, stating they have been notified that he doesn't have complete citizenship in the UK.)

DEVONTE. *(Reading the letter.)* "It's recently come to our attention: We have insufficient records of your residency in this country. You have up to two weeks to show legal documentation (passport, birth certificate). As a result, if unattainable, we may investigate further and could proceed with deportation to the country of birth."

(We see DEVONTE shift from a tense angry man to a defeated and scared boy as he reads the letter.)

(Devonte's world falls apart. He goes to rip the letter but stops himself, then places it in his pocket. He aims to hide this from his friends.)

ACT TWO

Time

(**DEVONTE** *centre stage seated by himself with the letter. It's pitch-black around him but he is clearly visible. A sound of a clock ticking begins to continuously play through the scene.*)

(**IMMIGRATION OFFICER** *is played by the actor who played* **PAUL**. *Throughout the meeting the* **IMMIGRATION OFFICER** *is taking notes.*)

IMMIGRATION OFFICER. Mr Devont Miller.

DEVONTE. Dee-von-tae. Yeah.

IMMIGRATION OFFICER. I'm just going to call you D for short. D, How are you doing, you alright? James Wardley, Immigration Officer.

(**DEVONTE** *stands and offers a handshake.*)

IMMIGRATION OFFICER. Take a seat. Just got a few questions.

(**DEVONTE** *sits.*)

DEVONTE. Why am I here?

IMMIGRATION OFFICER. Don't worry, you're not in trouble. Your information or should I say lack of, came up on our database. We just wanted to iron out a few things. So, shall we begin? It's August fifteenth 5.34 p.m.

(**DEVONTE** *nods.*)

Could you perhaps tell me where you are from?

DEVONTE. Peckham, South London.

IMMIGRATION OFFICER. Where are your parents from?

DEVONTE. Jamaica.

IMMIGRATION OFFICER. Jamaica, *Cool Runnings*, great film.

Were – you weren't born in the United Kingdom. Is that correct?

DEVONTE. Correct.

IMMIGRATION OFFICER. Could you provide us with your birth certificate?

DEVONTE. My mum should be able to sort all of this. She just not well at the moment.

IMMIGRATION OFFICER. Were you granted permission to stay in the UK?

DEVONTE. Permission? I've been here since I was nine years old.

IMMIGRATION OFFICER. You automatically become a UK citizen if you lived here for ten years. Looks like you were one year off that mark.

(Beat.)

Have you issued paperwork to confirm that you have status to be in the UK?

DEVONTE. What you talking about? I just finished my A-levels. I go to school here.

IMMIGRATION OFFICER. But you're technically not from here!

(Silence.)

Right, D, you seem like a bright kid. You shouldn't be up in all this mess. It's not your fault.

(Beat.)

Now I'm going to ask you a few more questions and I need you to answer this correctly. Do you understand?

(**DEVONTE** *nods.*)

Can you provide any paperwork to confirm that you've had status to be in the UK?

(*Pause.*)

DEVONTE. My national insurance number is...

IMMIGRATION OFFICER. That won't be necessary.

What's the purpose of your visit?

DEVONTE. Visit? I just told you. I live here.

IMMIGRATION OFFICER. If you wish to continue giving attitude, we will terminate this interview. I'll get someone else in and they won't be as friendly as me, alright.

(**DEVONTE** *defuses his flame.*)

Do you have a right to work in the UK?

DEVONTE. (*Confusedly.*) Yeah.

IMMIGRATION OFFICER. What's your occupation?

DEVONTE. Just finished College. I don't have a job. My Mum wanted me to focus on my studies.

IMMIGRATION OFFICER. So unemployed then.

(**DEVONTE** *shifts in his seat.*)

That's it for now. If we have any more questions we will be in touch.

Don't worry. You will be conpensated for your troubles. Everything is going to be alright.

DEVONTE. Can I go now?

(**IMMIGRATION OFFICER** *leaves.*)

Tunde's Eighteenth Birthday Party

(Adventure Youth Club hall.)

(Dancehall and Afrobeat music playing in the background.*)

*(**PAUL** and **TUNDE** have had a few drinks. **SALIM** hasn't.)*

SALIM. Oi this is sick, watch me nuh.

(Attempts to dance.)

PAUL. *(Laughs.)* What are you doing mate?

Me? I got the moves; I can whine mi waist and bubble to the beat. Oi Birthday boy T...Tunde

*(**TUNDE** is drunk and is dancing.)*

TUNDE. P money!!!!

PAUL. He's off his head he is. *(To **SALIM**.)* T. Who's a better dancer, me or Salim?

*(**TUNDE** isn't listening and is trying to focus on his dancing.)*

Tunde!

*(**PAUL** goes to tap **TUNDE** on the shoulder.)*

TUNDE. GBESE!!!

*(**TUNDE** attempts a Nigerian (Yoruba) dance move and falls flat onto the floor. **SALIM** laugh.)*

---

* A licence to produce *One Way Out* does not include a performance license for any third-party or copyrighted music. Licensees should create an original composition or use music in the public domain. For further information, please see the Music Use Note on page iii.

PAUL. Look at you, you plonker. Come here.

> (**PAUL** *helps* **TUNDE** *up and puts his arm around him.* **SALIM** *laughs.*)

TUNDE. I love you man.

PAUL. Yeah yeah come on let's get you sorted.

TUNDE. Na man, I love you, bro. You're like my best friend.

PAUL. Don't let Devonte hear you say that.

TUNDE. Bestie. Bestie.

PAUL. Alright, let get a move on.

> (*The song changes to K-Trap – "Warm".**)

TUNDE. Ayeee yo!! This is my tuneeee!

> (**TUNDE** *takes centre stage, as he lip-syncs to K-Trap – "Warm" [or any popular song of the time].* **SALIM & PAUL**, *wearing sunglasses, support him by flashing their light torches from their phones, creating a spotlight for a rap cypher aesthetic.*)

> (**DEVONTE** *enters, observing his friends from afar. He take his phone out to film them.*)

PAUL. DEVONTEE!!!

SALIM. Where you've been?

---

* A licence to produce *One Way Out* does not include a performance licence for K-Trap – "Warm". The publisher and author suggest that the licensee contact PRS to ascertain the music publisher and contact such music publisher to license or acquire permission for performance of the song. If a licence or permission is unattainable for K-Trap – "Warm", the licensee may not use the song in *One Way Out* but should create an original composition in a similar style or use a similar song in the public domain. For further information, please see the Music and Third-Party Materials Use Note on page iii.

DEVONTE. Couldn't miss my boy's eighteenth birthday, could I?

> (**TUNDE** *nods in acknowledgement.*)

Sorry about Results Day, just had a lot going on, init.

TUNDE. Sorry about what I said, I didn't know..

DEVONTE.	**TUNDE**.
We cool.	Yeah we cool? but I swear if you ever try bang me in my face again, I –

> (*The* **BOYS** *embrace in their familiar handshake, all the* **BOYS** *celebrate their return.*)

SALIM. Wow that's actually moving me to tears bro. Feel like Tunde after that punch.

TUNDE, DEVONTE & PAUL. Shut up Salim!!

PAUL. This is what friendship's about man it was all fragmented and now it's back together like pieces of a puzzle. It's magic.

> (*Beat.*)

DEVONTE. Yo! There are bare girls in the other room, looking for the birthday boy.

PAUL. Really?/

TUNDE. For me yeah?

> (**TUNDE & PAUL** *exit rapidly.*)

DEVONTE. Na I'm playing (*Laughs hysterically.*)

SALIM. Oi Devonte, my brother...

DEVONTE. What you telling me Salim?

SALIM. Did you mange to read that letter?

DEVONTE. Yeah. Nothing serious.

SALIM. Cool. How's Aunty Barbara?

DEVONTE. Getting by.

SALIM. Good to hear. Remember what my Uncle said, if you need anything, we got you.

>(**DEVONTE** *nods.* **PAUL & TUNDE** *enter.*)

PAUL. Oi! Guys, guess who's here?

SALIM. Who?

DEVONTE. Who

Wait.

TUNDE. It is...?

ALL. MICHAELAAAAAAAA!!!!!!!!

>(**BOYS** *get overly excited, jumping up and down like thrilled children. They embrace like they scored the winning goal in a cup final.*)
>
>(*Composure.*)
>
>(*All the* **BOYS** *look at each other as if they know it's time to dance with a girl.*)

TUNDE. I need to make sure I provide amazing hosp. hopila. Hospital –

PAUL. Hospitality.

TUNDE. Yeah, thank you. Best friend.

>(**TUNDE** *attempts to fist pump* **PAUL** *but loses balance.*)
>
>(**PAUL** *catches him.*)

PAUL. Woah! Easy there fella.

DEVONTE. Well you and your *best friend* should stay here, while *I* attend to Michaela.

SALIM. You think she's even gonna remember you.

DEVONTE.   Only time will tell. Ah she's such a Goddess, Michaela is so ridiculously peng, it's…ridiculous. A Nubian Queen and I'm gonna see if I can be her Prince Charming.

> (**DEVONTE** *goes to leaves.*)

Salim… Wanna be my backup dancer?

SALIM. Alright then.

> (*Both leave.*)

> (**PAUL** *puts* **TUNDE** *to sleep, carefully making sure he doesn't wake him up.* **PAUL** *decides to joins the party.*)

> (**DEVONTE**, **PAUL** *and* **SALIM** *are all dancing and enjoying the party. They begin to whine girls as Usher – "Nice and Slow" begins to play.* * *All the* **BOYS** *have different experiences.* **DEVONTE** *is pulled by…* **MICHAELA**.*)

DEVONTE. Michaela

The finest girl in college, wants to dance with me.

"I've missed you not being around. It's been such a longtime," she says.

I'm amazed because even though I know I'm good looking. This girl never speaks to me.

---

* A licence to produce *One Way Out* does not include a performance licence for Usher – "Nice and Slow". The publisher and author suggest that the licensee contact PRS to ascertain the music publisher and contact such music publisher to license or acquire permission for performance of the song. If a licence or permission is unattainable for Usher – "Nice and Slow", the licensee may not use the song in *One Way Out* but should create an original composition in a similar style or use a similar song in the public domain. For further information, please see the Music and Third-Party Materials Use Note on page iii.

Maybe it's true what they say: absence does make the heart go fonder.

In the shadows her face is so close to mine that I can smell the cocoa butter on her skin. "I don't know what it is you've done to me."

I can't figure out just what to do, when the cause and cure is you. We dance, no we are grinding to the sweet sound of nostalgic 90s R'n'B. Michaela turns around and elegantly places hers arms over my shoulders. Brushes my face ever so gently like a true artist creating a masterpiece.

Her eyes begin to close.

I lick my lips to prevent them being dry and crusty.

As our two heads close the space between them.

She kisses me.

I get so weak in the knees, I can hardly speak, I lose all control. In all honesty I had not invited this prodigy of a tongue; but we are now making out in the middle of the party, in the Youth Club. Oh I love this place. I'm gonna miss this place...

"Let's get out of here," she says.

My face lights up then suddenly dims as I'm trying to play it cool.

She pulls my hand, and directs us to the exit, as we weave through the moving bodies and the mask oursleves from the smell of sweat and cheap alcohol.

Today, I leave the Youth Club a Boy.

Tommorow I'll return as a Man.

(SWV – "Weak" plays.*)

*(**DEVONTE** exits, as he leaves hastily, he drops his deportation investigation letter.)*

*(**SALIM** searching for his boy, sees this and decides to pick it up and read it, he shares the news with **PAUL**. The **BOYS** are worried for their friend.)*

---

* A licence to produce *One Way Out* does not include a performance licence for SWV – "Weak". The publisher and author suggest that the licensee contact PRS to ascertain the music publisher and contact such music publisher to license or acquire permission for performance of the song. If a licence or permission is unattainable for SWV – "Weak", the licensee may not use the song in *One Way Out* but should create an original composition in a similar style or use a similar song in the public domain. For further information, please see the Music and Third-Party Materials Use Note on page iii.

Rally Up

(Montage of interviews.)

TUNDE. He's just an eighteen years boy!

(Montage of social media post, being sent to each other.)

PAUL. Have you seen this! Eighteen-year-old teen has been threatened with deportation to Jamaica.

(Montage of gathering the community.)

SALIM. Everyone meet us at the Home Office! Three p.m.

TUNDE, SALIM & PAUL. NO TO DEPORTATIONS!!!

Fight For Your Rights

(Royal Free Hosiptal, North London. Urology and Renal unit.)

*(**DEVONTE** is placed on a chair beside Aunty Barbara's hospital bed.)*

DEVONTE. How you getting on mum?

Ricky and all the boys send you their love.

Me and the boys were having a laugh about when you're looking for important documents you look under the mattress. I did just that. Couldn't find anything, Mum.

Where's my passport?

How comes this was never sorted?

My life, My future.

I don't know anybody in Jamaica. I don't think I could survive in Jamaica, I have no one there, all my family are here, my friends are here. How can they send someone to a country with no support, no family, no nothing.

I'm British. I was raised here. On all those forms right, what do I always tick. BLACK BRITISH. So how comes all of a sudden they can decide when a black person is no longer British. What does it even mean to be British? So what, I came here when I was a kid, this ain't fair man.

When you brought me over, didn't you think to sort this out? Just because you got your stay doesn't automatically mean I've got mine mum.

*(**DEVONTE** begins to cry.)*

Why is it just me?

I don't want to go. I don't want to go. Please mum, don't let them take me. Please, there must be a way out of this. There must be.

(Movement sequence all the **BOYS** *try to uplift* **DEVONTE**.*)*

ACT THREE

Justice for D

(The three activists **SALIM, PAUL & TUNDE** *lay on a road outside the Home Office immigration detention centre to prevent* **DEVONTE** *being put on a deportation flight to Jamaica.* **BOYS** *protesting with signs up 'Justice for D', 'Stop All Charter Flights'.)*

TUNDE. Guys I don't think we should be here. What if my mum sees me.

SALIM. I'm not giving up on Devonte.

PAUL. Relax Tunde, you've already had your party. I'm sure your mum's not gonna pre-order an ass beating for 'Mis-behaving'.

TUNDE. You don't know my mum.

SALIM. You man focus!

PAUL. So what do we do now.

SALIM. We sit here and wait till the deportation enquiry for Devonte is dropped.

PAUL. Right!!

    (Silence.)

Free my Bro!

TUNDE. He's not in Jail!!!

PAUL. Oh.

SALIM. What's the difference? I can't lie, deporting people who lived here most of there life is actually just proof that this country will do whatever it can to prove that it's racist.

BOYS. WE WANT REPARATIONS, NO TO DEPORTATIONS!

WE WANT REPARATIONS, NO TO DEPORTATIONS!

WE WANT REPARATIONS, NO TO DEPORTATIONS!

(Police lights and sirens appear.)

TUNDE. Guys we really need to stop, were causing a scene.

SALIM. That's the whole point. WE WANT REPARATIONS, NO TO DEPORTATIONS!

TUNDE. There must be a better way of handling this. Maybe I could speak to my mum, she could speak to her bosses and get this cleared. She knows Devonte.

SALIM. It's too late for that, can't you see they've already got him.

TUNDE. You know we could get arrested for public nuisance. Public nuisance is traditionally a criminal offence, defined as an unlawful act or omission which endangers or interferes with the lives, comfort, property or common rights of the general public. This is public property!!

PAUL. Yeah you don't say. WE WANT REPARATIONS, NO TO DEPORTATIONS!

TUNDE. I can't get a criminal record, I don't want to get kicked out of Uni, my future. My life would be ruined. I'd get sent back to Nigeria.

*(**TUNDE** attempts to leave.)*

SALIM. Tunde can you stop thinking about yourself for one second!!!

Your best friend needs you, why don't you care? Do you not understand if we don't do this, we may never see Devonte again.

TUNDE. I just don't think rioting is the right way. You don't understand, I can't make one mistake in this life. As a Black man you always gotta work twice as hard, that's what mum says. And I ain't tryna let her down now.

SALIM. We are taking action to prevent people like Devonte from being ripped away from their families, communities and loved ones. And these people are doing it twice as fast. This is bigger than us. Bigger than what any degree can give you. So fight for your brother man.

> (**TUNDE** *agrees to join. all three* **BOYS** *raise their banners, in a peaceful protest as the fight for* **DEVONTE** *continues.*)

Detained

DEVONTE. I was detained at Harmondsworth Immigration Removal Centre near London's Heathrow Airport.

They told me –

IMMIGRATION OFFICER. Everything is going to be fine.

DEVONTE. Me like an eediat believe them.

(Pause.)

Was waiting to hear back from my solicitor when they told me they wanted placed me on a one way flight straight back to Jamaica...

(Beat.)

Administrative removal they call it.

You're asked to leave because you've overstayed your permission to live in the UK.

It's funny right, our people were literally begged to come over here, build the country to what it is now. And all of a sudden we need permission to live here.

Seventy-five years.

It's been seventy-five years.

Funny how its, seventy-five years of windrush and seventy-five years of the NHS. I know I'm pretty good at maths but you work it out.

And of course the governemt do what them always do 'have an inquiry' inquiry about missing paperwork, inquiry about individual cases however whilst all of this is going on, them same people deporting all of us day in, day out.

(Beat.)

Why don't you people just leave us alone!

Dream Again

(We see **DEVONTE** *in a dream state, his current situation feels like a nightmare, his friends begin to feel like a distant figure in his memory... SWV – "Weak" plays again,* **DEVONTE** *is dreaming of the 'night' he had with Michaela. Music stops abruptly,* **DEVONTE** *has awaken in the dentention centre. He has fogotten his environment.)*

Goodbye Britain

>(**DEVONTE** *is sitting in the Harmondsworth Immigration Removal Centre, reading a book, to him it feels like prison. As he looks up, he sees* **TUNDE**. *They haven't seen each other in months.*)

IMMIGRATION OFFICER. Mr Miller, you've got a visitor.

>(*Enters* **TUNDE**.)

You've got five minutes.

>(*They both look at the* **OFFICER**, *insinuating him to leave.*)

Protocol.

TUNDE. Long time, no see.

DEVONTE. Been occupied.

>(*Beat.*)

You ever read the book *Frankenstein*?

TUNDE. Yeah why?

DEVONTE. What is it about?

TUNDE. A young scientist who creates a monster in an unorthodox scientific experiment.

DEVONTE. Ever notice the racial undertones?

TUNDE. Racial undertones?

DEVONTE. People are scared of the creature based on what it looks like. Prejudice against minorities.

TUNDE. But some of it bottles down to how we fight back

DEVONTE. What does that mean, if people are set up to fail they fail.

TUNDE. Not all of us fail

>   *(Beat.)*

DEVONTE. It's easy to judge from the outside, same way it's easy to judge the creature.

>   *(Beat.)*

>   *(**TUNDE** realises **DEVONTE** is talking about himself.)*

Everyone thinks the creature is a monster because of the way Frankenstein made him but maybe it's the way Frankenstein treated him that made him into a monster.

TUNDE. You still got it, don't you? Always had a way with words. You know the whole college started a protest, We've got Ricky. Michaela even Miss Wilson. They were all there, fighting for you...

>   *(**IMMIGRATION OFFICER** coughs as a sign to 'wrap it up'.)*

So is it definite then.

DEVONTE. Yeah, I leave in the morning. First class to Montego Bay airport.

TUNDE. Why didn't you tell us, sooner?

DEVONTE. I dunno... I was embarrassed. Felt 'totally humiliated' by my country. This country. Like I've been in a fight for months. But at least in a fight, there's a sense of control, right? With this...just unbelievable sense of betrayal.

TUNDE. This isn't right. *(To the **IMMIGRATION OFFICER**.)* He's grown up here his whole life.

DEVONTE. They don't see it like that. They see an immigrant. A foreigner. Intruder.

TUNDE. You are none of those things.

DEVONTE. I feel like I am.

IMMIGRATION OFFICER. Alright boys, come on.

TUNDE. I have to get back to Uni now. Before I go, I forgot to give you something.

>   (**TUNDE** *hands* **DEVONTE** *a letter. It's his A-level results.*)

DEVONTE. What is it?

TUNDE. Open it.

DEVONTE. A, B, B.

TUNDE. See! I always knew you could reach your potential.

>   (**DEVONTE** *ponders in guilt and cries.*)

IMMIGRATION OFFICER. We've got to wrap this up now.

DEVONTE. Tunde. Would you look after mum for me, yeah?

TUNDE. Aunty Barbara will have me at her service, I promise.

IMMIGRATION OFFICER. Time.

>   (*They do their handshake and embrace,* **DEVONTE** *is left only, for the final time in the UK.*)

Fun Fact

(Paul's House. **SALIM** *enters wearing a Jubba Thobe visiting to see his old friend.)*

PAUL. What you doing here?

SALIM. What, can't I come see my mate?

PAUL. Oi you look well sharp!

SALIM. Just came from the Mosque, I thought I'd stop by.

It's weird without –

PAUL. Yeah.

SALIM. How you coping? Devonte gone, Tunde in Uni.

PAUL. It's cool, it's our new reality now right?

SALIM. What happened to you being a magician?

PAUL. That's a little boy's dream.

*(***PAUL** *puts the cards away.)*

Salim, did your Uncle Abdul ever get back to you about the job vacancy?

SALIM. Ah yeah. He did.

PAUL. Sick!! So when can I start? Dad's been bollocking me since Result's Day and I need to get out of this place.

SALIM. Paul. He said it's just for family.

PAUL. Me and you are like brothers so –

SALIM. My family.

(Beat.)

Sorry bro. But if you send your CV I could pass it around.

PAUL. It's cool.

SALIM. You wanna know something?

PAUL. What?

SALIM.   Remember that time when, I laughed at you because you didn't know what dialysis was.

PAUL. Yeah, Aunty Barbara's kidney failure.

SALIM. Truth is, I didn't know what it meant either, I just didn't want to seem insensitive to Devonte.

PAUL. Oh and you thought it'll be alright if it was me, did ya.

I thought I was a right idiot I was.

SALIM. You're not man, that's why I'm here to say I'm sorry.

PAUL. For what?

SALIM. I dunno, for making you the scapegoat all the time.

PAUL. Apology accepted.

(They sit in silence.)

Salim? What's a scapegoat? Is that a type of curried mutton, because one time Aunty Barbara made that for me and I swear on David Bowie's life I've never tasted anything so tantalsing in my life.

SALIM. OH MY DAYYYS YOU EEIIDIAT!

(They laugh.)

*(They do their handshake. **PAUL** reacts in pain.)*

What happened to your hand?

PAUL. Oh nothing.

SALIM. Doesn't look like nothing. Did you get into a fight, cos I swear I'll back it you know.

PAUL. Just my dad.

SALIM. Your dad?

PAUL. I just don't understand him.

Works all day then drinks all night, then gets back up again for work. and when he's tired and frustrated, guess who becomes the punching bag.

But not this time.

I hit him. Hard.

He called me useless, thick and he said I was a disappointment of a son. All because I wanted to do magic.

You'd think your kid having a passion for something would spark joy into your life but no.

Not him. How do you think I feel growing up seeing you piss yourself, wearing the same clothes every day. Not showering and slurring your words till the point you can't even form a sentence. As long as you know how to count your name and spell money, you'd be alright Son. Well I'm not alright, whilst he was off his head, binging I had to step up, get a real job, just like he wanted. Turns out scraping A-level maths came in handy. signed up for an apprentice scheme as a construction worker. Can you believe it!

    (Beat.)

Salim, am I the problem that he's trying to fix?

Devonte's One Way Home

(**DEVONTE** *is flowered with letters from family and friends, we see an Arsenal 'Jamaica Independence' football shirt, gifted to him by* **SALIM**.)

(**DEVONTE** *reads the letter.*)

SALIM. Hey, when you get to Jamaica make sure you tell the girls about me.

DEVONTE. *(Laughs.)* Yeah I will.

SALIM. *(Attempts patois.)* Tell them me is ah Coolie bwoy from foreign.

DEVONTE. Leave it out yeah Salim.

(*Both* **BOYS** *laugh off the awkwardness.*)

PAUL. You better pick up that phone when I need help with trigonometry.

My yute!

TUNDE. Not having you as a wingman in Uni is hard bro. I know you will be good out there, you always have been. Keep faith. I love you bro, remember that.

(**DEVONTE** *folds all the letters received, and take one last look of his environment. As he future is destined for Jamaica he exits.*)

Fate

SALIM. So you wanna know what it amounts to?

PAUL. Let me guess.

TUNDE. After he left…

PAUL. I was a bit naive.

SALIM. I'm moving up in the world,

PAUL. I thought we would all get a place together. Start a business or something.

SALIM. Uncle Abdul expanded yeah…

PAUL. Camberwell.

SALIM. Old Kent Road.

TUNDE. The 'Peckham'.

PAUL. Tunde? Yeah, Yeah, Tunde's doing great! He's at Uni.

TUNDE. A part of me wants to take a break, take a gap year.

SALIM. Put me in charge.

TUNDE. But mum isn't too pleased about that. And she's right. I've just got to keep my head down, and focus on making it through. I can't deviate from the plan, it's always been the plan. Something in a suit. it's a new chapter init, a lot to get used to.

SALIM. I've been focusing on my deen as well.

PAUL. Picked up a construction apprenticeship.

TUNDE. New environment.

SALIM. I feel like I'm gaining something there, the mosque.

TUNDE. New people.

PAUL. I started performing card tricks on site, people love it. They call me MAGIC PAUL! It's nice…

TUNDE. But no one's like my old friends.

SALIM. The whole thing with D – It just made me think. I realised, I didn't know what my community was.

PAUL. Building flats. It's nice. I work /

TUNDE. Hard. work hard. Don't question it. Get through it.

SALIM. We all put up the best fight to keep Devonte here.

PAUL. They say you don't know it's the best times till it's over.

SALIM. It could have been anyone.

TUNDE. Salim took it the hardest I think.

SALIM. I just wish I knew earlier.

TUNDE. Keep my head down. I just need to reach out.

SALIM. He still owes me £3.60 you know.

PAUL. How am I eighteen, and I've already run out time /

SALIM. Time. I don't really have the time.

TUNDE. To call.

PAUL. The connection is bad.

SALIM. It's all Whatsapp.

TUNDE. Memes.

PAUL. Gifs.

SALIM. Gifs.

TUNDE. Another world.

SALIM. I miss him, still. At the end of the day it all came to nothing.

TUNDE. The tweets.

SALIM. Posts.

PAUL. Protest.

SALIM. Absolutely nothing.

TUNDE. It's mad because they say he we wont be able to return to the UK for ten years.

PAUL. Ten years.

TUNDE. Like he's some sort of criminal.

SALIM. Excluded from society like he wasn't worth being here.

PAUL. One step for man.

ALL. A giant step back for the mandem.

> *(Beat.)*
>
> *(The three* **BOYS** *who have now turned into young men, clock each other.)*
>
> *(They all put their focus on the empty chair, 'Devonte's Chair', reminiscing their dear friend.)*
>
> *(Devonte.)*

TUNDE. Can I go now?

> *(Blackout.)*

The End